Blessings the Body Gave

Winner of the 1998 Ohio State University Press/
The Journal Award in Poetry

Blessings the Body Gave

WALT McDONALD

Ohio State University Press

Columbus

Library of Congress Cataloging-in-Publication Data
McDonald, Walter.
 Blessings the body gave / Walt McDonald.
  p.   cm.
 ISBN 0-8142-0804-5 (cloth : alk. paper). — ISBN 0-8142-5004-1
(paper : alk. paper)
 I. Title.
PS3563.A2914B54   1998
811'.54—dc21   98-29035
                                                  CIP

Text design by Will Underwood.
Jacket design by Gore Studio Inc.
Type set in Fairfield by Will Underwood.
Printed by Braun-Brumfield, Inc.

The paper used in this publication meets the minimum requirements of
the American National Standard for Information Sciences—Permanence
of Paper for Printed Library Materials.ANSI Z39.48-1992.

9 8 7 6 5 4 3 2 1

ACKNOWLEDGMENTS

I'm grateful to the following publications in which earlier versions
of these poems first appeared, some with different titles:

The American Scholar: "Anniversary: One Fine Day," "Losing It
   Again in Bozeman"
Bellowing Ark: "Song for One-Armed Cowboys"
The Boston Review: "Uncle Douglas and the Whirring Blades"
Buffalo Spree Magazine: "A Cabin, Even a Cave," "With Mercy for
   All"
The Christian Century: "Adoption"
Christianity and Literature: "That Child Abandoned on the Porch"
College English: "Grandfather's Pocket Watch"
Connecticut River Review: "For Donavon, Missing in Action"
The Cresset: "Alone in the Tundra"
Dalhousie Review (Canada): "River of the Arms of God"
Defined Providence: "Again This Winter"
Dictionary of Literary Biography: "In Dickey Country"
Envoi (U.K.): "East of Eden," "The First Months Home," Part 1
First Things: "Catching My Grandson," "The Waltz We Were Born
   For"
The Formalist: "After the Lost War," "How It's Done"
The Gettysburg Review: "Praying for Rain on the Plains," "The War
   in Bosnia," "Whatever It Takes"
Hubbub: "Weeding the Strawberry Garden"
JAMA: The Journal of the American Medical Association: "Sympathy"
The Kenyon Review: "Halfway between the Gulf and Mountains,"
   "My Father on His Shield," "The Winter They Bombed Pearl
   Harbor"
The Literary Review: "Wild Ducks Floating By"
London Review of Books (U.K.): "Uncle Earl's Wind River Ranch"
Many Mountains Moving: "To Have and to Hold," "Uncle Bill and
   Guns"
Maryland Poetry Review: "Blessings the Body Gave"

The Missouri Review: "After the Fires We Once Called Vietnam,"
"Cataracts," "Fishing with Uncle Walter in World War II,"
"Twins and Oral History," "Where Buffalo Grass Grows Loud If
We Listen"

The New Criterion: "Before Children"

New Letters: "Leaving the Scene," "When the Children Have Gone"

New Texas 98: "Traveling in Packs"

Nightsun: "The First Months Home," Part 2

North Dakota Quarterly: "For God in My Sorrows"

The Ohio Review: "Voices on Jukebox Wax"

Pembroke Magazine: "The Fox All Winter Long"

Poet Lore: "In Gusty Winds That Wild"

Poetry: "Old Pets"

Poetry East: "Cars Flash by on the Highway"

Prairie Schooner: "Fathers and Sons"

Seneca Review: "Baptizing the Dog at Nine"

The Sewanee Review: "Crossing the Road," "The Night I Left the
Air Force," "1945," "Spitfire," "Where the Fence Goes"

The Southern Review: "Jogging with Oscar"

Southern Poetry Review: "All We Do Is Already History"

Southwest Review: "Stones Grandfathers Carved"

Stand Magazine (U.K.): "What Old Pilots Say"

The Texas Review: "One Summer before Saigon"

Visions: "Aunt Linda and the Pink Bikini"

Windsor Review (Canada): "Learning How in the Southwest"

Writers' Forum: "The Moves a Body Makes"

"Anniversary: One Fine Day" is reprinted from *The American
Scholar*, volume 65, number 3, 1996. Copyright 1996 by Walter
McDonald. By permission of the publishers.

"Losing It Again in Bozeman" is reprinted from *The American
Scholar*, 1998. Copyright 1998 by Walter McDonald. By
permission of the publishers.

"Old Pets" was first published in *Poetry*. Copyright 1998 by the
Modern Poetry Association.

"Fathers and Sons" is reprinted from *Prairie Schooner* by permission
of University of Nebraska Press. Copyright 1997 by University of
Nebraska Press.

"Where the Fence Goes" (as "Mending Fence on Hardscrabble")
was published in *The Sewanee Review*, volume 101, number 1,
1993. Copyright 1993 by Walter McDonald.

"Crossing the Road" and "Spitfire" were published in *The Sewanee
Review*, volume 104, number 1, 1996. Copyright 1996 by Walter
McDonald.

"The Night I Left the Air Force" and "1945" were published in *The
Sewanee Review*, 1998. Copyright 1998 by Walter McDonald.

"Grandfather's Pocket Watch," formerly "Father's Pocket Watch,"
copyright 1995 by the National Council of Teachers of English.
Reprinted by permission of the publisher.

I'm especially grateful to Texas Tech University for time to write
many of these poems.

CONTENTS

Five: THE WALTZ WE WERE BORN FOR

One

CROSSING THE ROAD

MY FATHER ON HIS SHIELD

Shiny as wax, the cracked veneer Scotch-taped
and brittle. I can't bring my father back.
Legs crossed, he sits there brash

with a private's stripe, a world away
from the war they would ship him to
within days. Cannons flank his face

and banners above him like the flag
my mother kept on the mantel, folded tight,
white stars sharp-pointed on a field of blue.

I remember his fists, the iron he pounded,
five-pound hammer ringing steel,
the frame he made for a sled that winter

before the war. I remember the rope in his fist
around my chest, his other fist
shoving the snow, and downhill we dived,

his boots by my boots on the tongue,
pines whishing by, ice in my eyes, blinking
and squealing. I remember the troop train,

steam billowing like a smoke screen.
I remember wrecking the sled weeks later
and pounding to beat the iron flat,

but it stayed there bent
and stacked in the barn by the anvil,
and I can't bring him back.

THE WINTER THEY BOMBED
PEARL HARBOR

All winter peacocks screamed, strutting the same
slow pose. At dawn, we smashed the ice with hammers,
dumped pots of boiling water steaming into troughs
for beaks of preening peacocks. They shoved each other off
like cousins bunched at the only mirror at church.

My logger father whittled a forest with buzz saws,
the roar and buzz of steel and mosquitoes
more than my ears were tuned for.
My sister and I played keep-away with feathers,
dazzling the surly turkeys and peacocks with footwork,

lobbing frozen dirt clods like grenades,
until our father called us. When roads were frozen,
I jockeyed the throttle of a John Deere
rusted before the war, hauling logs and hay bales
to farmers miles away. The war was almost lost

when my father enlisted, Pearl Harbor bombed,
the fall of Bataan all we heard for hours
on every station at night, except for our parents
talking softly after bedtime
and peacocks screaming in the dark.

CROSSING THE ROAD

What's a boy to do, both shoes caught in the tar,
the road past our house turning to street,
and me, a chicken trying to reach the other side.
Men burly as uncles swore and shook their shovels,

laughing. My mother waited on the porch,
drying her hands in her apron. My big sister teased,
her gawky girlfriends howled, and someone screamed
Tar baby! I swear I tugged, cursing the only words

I had learned, squashed down in July asphalt
like a bug, like Captain Marvel in the comics
turned into a tree, unable to budge. And of all days,
on my birthday. Carl would see me soon, and Mary Jane,

all kids I knew pointing on the curb and dancing.
Like God roaring up on his motorcycle, my brother
dismounted and stared. Tucking a Camel in his lips,
he lit and flipped the match away, came strolling down,

fists doubled, snorting smoke, not smiling.
Massive, towering above me, he jerked me up
without my shoes and hauled me like a sack of oats
back to the grass, his own boots ruined.

I remember him that way, not the box of belongings
they brought from Okinawa, not the flag Mother hung
in the window for all cars to see speeding past
the four-lane street, pounding my sneakers down.

UNCLE DOUGLAS AND
THE WHIRRING BLADES

Uncle Douglas scolded my sister and me
for dawdling, called us his pests
and teased us, big knuckles
thumping our skulls like drums,

then whisked candy canes
out of our ears and armpits.
Uncle Douglas fattened pigs for market.
His windmill pumped sweet water

to the troughs and slaughter barn,
hundreds of chubby pigs grunting
and bumping buckets of grain and slop.
His dark eyes crossed and uncrossed,

his hairy nostrils wheezed—Wolf snout,
my sister whispered one night—
the wolf that puffed the pigs' house down
and ate them. If he's a wolf,

I wondered, where is his tail?
She cursed me, Dummy, under his coveralls.
Look how fat his bottom is, his belly:
he eats little nephews. Lie down

and go to sleep. All night the windmill
groaned and rattled, the squeal
of whirring blades, the room so dark
I swore he was at the door.

BAPTIZING THE DOG AT NINE

I heard puppies have no souls,
but I loved that mongrel with a bulldog mom.
Behind the barn, I preached that dog's head down
until he dozed. His stubby tail said *Yes, I believe
whatever you say.* Crows in the arbor cawed like scoffers.

I staggered with thirty grunting pounds, shoved him
to the stock tank and huffing said the words
and dumped him. He splashed and came up paddling,
head up and wholly dunked, shock of pond scum
in his eyes. The startled crows swirled off,

a flutter of black hosannahs. I thought he'd rise
and talk like Balaam's donkey, but he thrashed
as if drowning. Slick-haired, he never barked.
I had to drag him out, his glazed eyes hopeless,
fat crows in the arbor cawing.

1945

Nothing consoled Aunt Rose when Roosevelt died,
the war in Germany not won, but almost.
Even Uncle Oscar, rocking and swatting flies,
grumbled we'd win, with or without his ghost,
Roosevelt only the President, not God.
Aunt Rose wailed and begged him to hush,
squeezing a towel and weeping hard
as if another nephew died, flushed,

my mother fanning her. I had seen guys
across the road, spitting and kicking dust,
almost enough for a game and about my size,
but Mother made me go, always the first
dragged anywhere, flags at half mast, school out
for the day as if it snowed. What did I know,
me the baby in the family. Pouting
on their front porch, I tired to ignore

Aunt Rose's weeping, my mother's solace,
Uncle Oscar's constant rocking. Always
they scolded me for pulling blossoms,
but not that time: since I couldn't play,
I stripped the honeysuckle bare and sipped
the sweet, ripped all white flowers and flipped
confetti at the hound. What was the President
to me? Years before TV, when newsreels meant

nothing but boredom before the show—
always the war, a man's voice telling what we all
could see—troops going ashore in landing boats,
long shots of battleships, trained dogs
on water skies, bathing beauties as old
as my sisters. They never showed the man
with the newsreel voice, like radio
fireside chats. That year, Grandfather began

his eternal tinkering at dark
with whatever had to be fixed, but he always
turned it louder than any ballpark
broadcast he ever let me hear, his face
strained and listening, Grandfather suddenly old—
the President's failing voice in our own living room—
as if he hoped we'd hear it would all be over soon,
how my uncles were, when they'd be coming home.

UNCLE BILL AND GUNS

No one loved guns like Uncle Bill,
barrel-chested and fifty, too old for World War II.
He hated being alone, his mountain woods so quiet
he praised the wings of owls. His cabin was a mansion
of trophies, old heads of moose and rams,

four grizzlies he swore he killed with pistols.
He kept guns loaded for us, his summer nephews.
Mother warned us about his wandering
after Aunt Ethel's death in a car wreck,
his squandered fortune, his dozen jungle safaris.

But Bill told stories we wanted, wore bracelets of rattles,
a loop of fangs as an earring. Our mother frowned,
worried we'd follow, get shot and rot in a canyon.
He taught us to draw, that slap of leather
and wavering whine through a valley.

He taught us load and lock, how to survive
with only pistols and bedrolls, sipping bourbon
with Uncle Bill, his back to the campfire,
shouting, tossing rocks at the dark,
daring anything to strike.

AUNT LINDA AND THE PINK BIKINI

Her tongue was spice and lightning
even at nineteen. She caught her husband
playing doctor with a nurse and cursed him,
calling all doctors frauds. She kept his name

for herself, the cars and house for their children.
She sold most stocks for a wardrobe. In time,
Cadillacs came by, Mercedes, pickups with gun racks—
I couldn't count the cowboy boots that strutted

to her door. Men liked her summer laugh,
pink thongs and terry cloth. I remember Aunt Linda
in bikinis at picnics, divorced in-law, but family.
I was bold with mustard for her burgers,

the perfect nephew. Linda always had a sticky kiss
for me, and whispered six-packs of advice—*Shave close
and take no prisoners*. She clipped me on the chin
and left sweet lipstick on my cheek. One year,

I listened hard and heard Aunt Linda whisper vows
in a veil Uncle Cal lifted—she made me call
the tall cowboy that—and he kissed her
glistening lips, and all the family sighed.

CARS FLASH BY ON THE HIGHWAY

Billy Ray tilted his deer-hide chair and stretched,
stiff after hours in a saddle. Any stone café was home
after a week of roundup. We needed fiddles
and jukebox steel guitars, nothing better than a waitress

with a fist of steam and a menu. I heard steaks sizzle,
the rattle of pans in the kitchen. Hot baths tonight
and a barn dance, five hours till midnight
when local girls drove pickups home.

Sipping cold coffee, I watched cars flash by
on the highway—my birthday tomorrow, old enough
to buy beer legally at last, to register for the draft,
to get my license and go wherever I wanted to go.

Two

SPITFIRE

FOR DONAVON, MISSING IN ACTION

Booze and a dance band swore I was older,
and crepe-paper streamers twisted
tight over all who soloed
in the squadron that night, fists
whacking our backs and buddies shouting.
Instructor pilots gaudy as lions
leaned back and watched wives dancing,
sun glasses cocked down from their eyes,
scarves fluffed at their throats,
heroes we worshiped but swore
we could beat one on one, someday.
Maracas and trumpets blasted our dates
to our arms, so loud we surrendered
gladly, tossing down blue flames
of brandy, repeating words we'd heard
like *love,* coupled to their sweet names

until lights went out all over Georgia,
party over at dawn. At dawn, we crawled
down into cockpits, a melodrama
of masks, pure oxygen before roll call,
as long as they'll let us, all dials
and gauges in the green, controls
still working. There was the sky
bright as ever, after my first night solo,
the fear of mystery gone,
back into the skies. I might have wished
for years of peace, knowing real wars
might come with others who'd risk anything,
who knew the thrill and reason for this,
but with enemy symbols on their wings.

ONE SUMMER BEFORE SAIGON

Blood toothed and beady eyed, our squadron arm patch
had no name but numbers, 683, the beast on wings
above the enemy. Some woman stitched them blue and crimson,
rockets like silver spears. One day I saw her house, gables

and a picket fence, a porch swing in a neighborhood of lawns
and hundred-year-old trees, an arboretum with azaleas
and dogwood blossoms white as a bride's bouquet.
Conrad and I passed by to meet some neighbor's daughter

and her friend, smooth-shouldered local girls
with breath like cigarettes and wrinkled eyes, cashiers
who dated hundreds of pilots before us. That night
we talked about hobbies and fast cars, exotic places on the map

they'd like to live. Our pilot hands showed them
the latest moves to roll and race away from bad guys
in the sky, to turn and slide behind them for a shot.
They taught us touch and counterturn, moves they'd learned

from others. I wondered if they helped stitch patches
after hours, if they knew all squadron mottos and call signs,
if our seamstress had dated pilots in World War II,
if she ever wept when one by one they died or disappeared,

which local boy she married, if she had daughters,
what she thought about inside her parlor rocking,
her nimble fingers stitching our mascot's skull and fangs,
jerking the needle through and down into the eyes.

THE FOX ALL WINTER LONG

How cautiously it's done,
crouch with one paw tucked,
and pounce. The fox
eats the field mouse
with its teeth bared,
fast little bites
as if it's bitter,
the mouse tail stiff,
flicking like a toothpick.
Swallows, looks around
like a schoolboy finding a dime,
trots on, hoping
to find more coins,
a hole in somebody's pocket.
The fox all winter listens
with one ear to the wind, hops
on the slightest sound,
burrows down to the fastest,
tiny feet, cold grass
no match for a fox
that survives mountain lions,
sometimes even eagles
that can hear fox paws
pounce and pounce.

MARRIAGE IS A BUNGEE JUMP

Marriage is a bungee jump off some box canyon
in Colorado, concession manned by a minion
from the fifties high on weed, beard he hadn't brushed
since high school. The ropes felt new enough

and he swore he measured them, the fall to the rocks
a lovers' leap eighty stories long.
He made us sign a waiver and pay in cash.
Folding the bills away, he slouched back to the shack

and high-fived a friend who passed the bottle back—
Done it again, like cupid. We heard a match strike,
the sizzle of hemp. We checked the ropes, the stiff knots
tied by someone who flunked that lesson in scouts.

We'd checked the charts, the geology of cliffs
and canyons, but no one knows which fibers split,
which granite ledges crack. On the edge of hope
for nothing we'd ever done, we tugged at the ropes,

both ropes, blessing the stretch and strain
with our bodies, a long time falling to the pain
and certainly of stop. Hand in hand we stepped up
wavering to the ledge, hearing the rush

of a river we leaped to, a far-off
cawing crow, the primitive breeze of the fall,
and squeezed, clinging to each other's vows
that only death could separate us now.

UNCLE EARL'S WIND RIVER RANCH

It's salt, not rain, fat elk cows need. Uncle Earl
hauls salt blocks up from town and dumps them, wedged
by boulders licking tongues can't tumble.
Elk wander down to graze his slope. Wild elk
never nod, big bellies swaying, calves on their way,
most snow melted that far down in gusty winds
that wild. Uncle Earl looks up maybe once a day,
takes elk for granted and boulders above him,
a million years of rocky mountain balanced
except stones that tumbled, an avalanche of chance.

Like that one massive as his barn, a stone
he built his wide corral around. Look at those
up there, a thousand boulders propped on slate
and sand that slides, erodes, steep ledges cracked
and tilted where cougars make their homes,
scratching gravel to widen cracks for caves,
arching their long big-muscled backs.

BEFORE CHILDREN

We rose from the snow
where we rooted for truffles
lost in the leaves hogs missed,
gouging fluffed mounds like plows.
With gloves, we never found them,
frozen like trout. We knew they were there,
somewhere, locked in a vault of ice.
Stripped to our thumbs, we dug
till our nails would have bled
but for the cold, hoping to find
more truffles ripe as dark chocolate,
the centers soft, tangy as chestnuts
roasting all day in a cabin
where at night we thawed our fists
and tips of noses up close,
the smoke of piñon and taste of truffles
worth hours without gloves,
stiff fingers starting to flex.

ADOPTION

We took them in our arms, those washed,
donated blankets and week-old babies,
bare facts scratched on tablet paper—
their foster parents' chronicles
of formula and colic, their bottles
and pajamas, their oddly temporary names.

Three babies in different years, the lightest loads
we'd ever hold. That was the Sixties
before I went to Vietnam and back,
branded vicious, a baby killer. Such hope
never happened again, the whole world's peace
at risk. Those wise caseworkers knew about loss,

half trauma nurses, half Santa Claus.
Joyful, we took the babies they gave,
miraculous heartbreak, each almost weightless,
shockingly small, almost too delicate to take
from the arms of a woman who knew how to bring
and let go. I can still feel the cling

of fingers wrapped around mine,
the charm of tiny eyes squeezed tight.
We held each baby in the neon gaze
of the state's agency, helpless, tall,
heart-pounding strangers these babies came to—
voices they'd never heard, might never

have picked—big-fisted, dazed,
throat-choked and humming lullabies,
blur-eyed, not caring who might see.
We were only a couple holding a baby
giddy and trembling with questions, and clumsy,
but parents, and our baby was crying.

WHAT OLD PILOTS SAY

Play with it, say it out loud when you're alone,
if that will help. Gnaw horror like a bone,
suck blood and marrow out. Reach behind your face
and turn it off, like lights-out on the base.
Someone will die today, tonight. Rockets fall,
some posts get overrun. That's what the guards
and body bags are for. You can't fly without sleep.
Tell your first sergeant, *Wake me*
if they break through the lines. Otherwise
let it lie. Take it one flight at a time.

Home won't come by holding your balls
and breath too tightly in your fist. Jog,
play handball, cut back on booze and easy lays
after you're back. Look both ways
in Asian skies, swivel your crash-helmet head.
When your wingman spots a missile, break
any way he says. One flight at a time.
Go back to the world, your only wife,
breed lots of kids and tell your lies.
Or not. Some of us have to die.

ROCKET ATTACK

Crack like a screen door slammed
and cannon fire. After that first explosion,
silence, then fallout that clattered down.
I heard shouts and sirens and saw men run,

the roar of choppers and gunfire at dawn,
the rumble of bombs. I remember the weird
thrill of falling hard as they taught,
someone throwing up next door in fear.

I remember waking later, stunned that I slept
after that. I followed echoes in my skull
to the shattered hootch, airmen dead
in a crater fifty feet east—their blood

splattered like motor oil. MP's stood guard,
and corpsmen sifted smoking dirt for bones
or flesh. I remember breakfast was lard
and runny eggs with ketchup and burned toast

butter-soaked, and bacon fried soggy
in a tent reeking of greasy smoke and wood.
It seemed insane—*but the fragile body
was hungry, and it was good, it tasted good.*

THE TRACK AT SAIGON

We jogged fast laps on asphalt
flat as a runway, counting rumors of riots
back home, divorces, nights without rockets.

We tried staying sober in daylight,
hard to worry stripped down to shorts,
gasping, drenched in sunburn and sweat

to keep our bodies hard. We heard
the thud and quiver of a high board
across the fence, a sudden splash,

laughter of French landowners by a pool.
At dawn, while corpsmen loaded body bags,
we ran in a world exploding—

thunder of jets loaded with napalm,
whop whop of choppers lifting wounded
from the front, the nearby boom of bombs.

MY COUSIN AND THE V.A. NURSE

It isn't easy, swinging dead legs,
but Carlin does it, flinging that walker along,
clop clop, then shifting both legs, a gallop
on balanced aluminum sticks with rubber boots.

Before the war he never walked
when he could ride horseback or climb
steep mountains, diving into deep,
clear canyon pools, my cousin from Montana

who went Airborne before eighteen.
Rangers taught him to walk and crawl
through jungles, how to pause and play dead
for hours, then wiggle off like a moccasin

through swamps. Months later, nurses taught him
to call for help from a bed, to squeeze
the toggle switch and turn a wheelchair
down the corridor without landmines,

to open doors, where Carlin stalled one day
down a ramp and tumbled, the battery dead,
beating the wheels until his knuckles bled,
until one young nurse came running

in a starched white dress, rushing toward him
from a stunning, sun-lit garden, white cap,
even her shoes and stockings white, running
with arms out wide and calling, calling his name.

THE FIRST MONTHS HOME

I

That black bear, ravenous, slaps her great paw down,
down, and the bough breaks. Food they tied in a pouch
crashes at her feet, glass shatters, aroma of yeast
and onions even we can sniff, a feast of bread and cheese.
We watch from our car, seeing the tent twenty feet away.
Silhouettes inside on their knees hump and sway
as if having sex. Through their zipped mosquito net
they see their paltry food, not enough to satisfy one bear,
paws able to rip their tent with a slash of claws,
jaws the size of thighs. Are we fools to follow laws?
Hang food in trees away from bears, from the bed you share
with someone you love. All's fair to this bear.

After mauling the sack and grease spots on the ground,
she waddles off. Still frightened, they crawl out,
like buddies in bunkers after the siren wailed
all clear and only the radio corporal declared
Saigon safe at last—a dispatch some sergeant wrote
and shoved under his nose, all of us knowing
no one could know if rockets aimed at us
ten miles out in the jungle, if VC gunners
crouched down now to fire them, or if they'd slide
deep into tunnels until tomorrow night.

2

Not even twelve, but up, beside her in the bed,
amazed and watching shadows, the same moon
haunted by the hour. I can't keep it out, drapes drawn,
storm shutters tight. Our children sleep, well fed
and glad their daddy's back. It's midnight in the bones.
They're out there, somewhere, flogging the horse

gone lame, cart wheel broken off the shaft.
They'll come, somehow, floating on skiffs of eyelids
they've ripped and stitched. I want to kill.
The kitchen floor blinks bright and widens back.
Door opened, the light stays on. Closed, the fridge
is always dark, shut tight and always chilled,

but dark. I take a bottle and softly close the door.
The sweet, clean, bitter taste of hops makes it all right
for now, the bottle cold and sweaty to the touch.
I count the hours to daylight: too much to do tomorrow
not to sleep, too much. They're out there tonight
like sappers. By now, they've killed the horse. So much

at night is Vietnam. I drain the beer in the sink
and listen, straining, the sizzle of foam like fire.
By now, they've found the gate. The motor clicks
and whirs, too loud, to keep the next beer cold.
Listen: is that the twang of barbed wires
in the yard, the creak of footsteps on the porch?

WITH MERCY FOR ALL

She was a mystery of give and take,
laid open to strangers and neighbors in need,
no thought of lawsuits in those innocent days.
She took abuse from people she helped feed
in the Texas depression, who quarreled
and promised to pay her back, but frowned
and walked away when they saw her
after church. Our mother never doubted
evil was merely need in neighbors.
She carried fables with her to the grave,
although she saw her father pistol-whipped
for giving a man a ride in winter.
A thousand nights she sat with the aged,
the sick and the dying. At thirty-eight,
she ran bare-footed to save a child,
jerking him up from the screaming mother
and pumping the marble out. Then collapsed in the briars
coming back, had to be helped home by others.
My sister tweezered sixty stickers from her feet.
Mother moaned how thankful she missed them
going over, though dozens stuck to her feet
when she ran to that baby on adrenaline
and faith. She never fathomed how pluck happened
throughout her life, how fast it left her
lovely and flushed, trembling with a funeral fan
in her hand, a comely woman, mother, nurse,
who believed herself simple, submissive, afraid,
not knowing how able she was, how recklessly brave.

SPITFIRE

The first week the prop leaked oil, old engine grimy
no matter how much I scrubbed, down on my knees
or flat on my back, jabbing at cracks with rags.
All week I flew jets and tinkered with the relic,
the Battle of Britain almost forgotten. For months
I pumped iron, jerking at bolts frozen by rust,

sticking my wrench into slits by the magneto, tugging at nuts
that wouldn't budge. Stingy, they loosened with hard work
and luck, like seams giving up their gold to only the rude,
the desperate. I'd break my knuckles to make that Spitfire fly,
built before I was born, burned out, most canopy rivets cracked.
When my bride took the knife and sliced the cake

with my hand over hers, my nails were swarthy no matter
how much I scrubbed. For months she came back from town
and found me already hot in the garage, buffing,
scrubbing some valve, inserting some scarce part
that came by mail. And then the children, the playpen,
boxes of toys and rocker horses outgrown, stacked in the closet.

For years I ducked and crawled under, an hour now and then,
a few minutes on weekends, taking gauges apart
that worked a year ago, tires flat again, canopy caked
by barn owls, the war on all the channels.
I came back from Saigon to hold my wife, each child,
went madly back to work. Nights, I tuned the engine

in the family wagon with the cracked windshield,
drove children to practice, gave away broken toys
and sold the picket fence. Old friends kept dropping by,
some on their way overseas, most back from Vietnam
with medals on their chests, testing the Spitfire's metal,
thumping the tires, rubbing the fuselage, the prop.

One night when I was down on my knees looking for clues,
Carl came with his checkbook and truck, and when he left,
the Spitfire followed like a dog with hind legs bound,
dragged down the winding mountain road.

THE NIGHT I LEFT THE AIR FORCE

Moving is all we ever do, our daughter cried,
fists in her armpits, weeping. Five homes
in seven years, like bridges burned. The light
by her bed was on, her mother and I drowsy
in the blinding light, squinting, tying our robes.
My wife sat close to hold her. Soon, she was out

again, our frightened girl, and I switched out the light.
Back from Saigon, I watched good friends taking off
and turned my flight suits back in, after my last flight
was grounded by an engine fire. If not delayed
an hour by weather, I might have crashed on takeoff.
I never flew again, my orders approved that day,

the movers due at dawn. We boxed my uniforms and boots,
the flag and half my life, no more a pilot than our girl.
Where will we go? she asked while Jimmy stared, not rude
but mute, mouth open, another puzzled child she'd lost.
Her home meant friends like Jimmy, the world to her
vaguely dangerous, where Daddy once had gone, his war

on all the channels. Hugged and tucked into bed,
the night-light on, even fat bears to comfort her,
she may have stared at TV pictures in her head,
seen soldiers big as her daddy dying soon,
monks burning in the streets, little girls like her
running lost and screaming in our living room.

Three

TRAVELING IN PACKS

HALFWAY BETWEEN THE GULF
AND MOUNTAINS

We memorized each other's eyes before Saigon,
casting for bass after dark, hearing the splash
and battle in the shallows. Driving back, we watched hawks
glide over piñon and spruce and disappear.
I rode the brakes around steep switchbacks.

Centuries slid past the last wide turns.
We saw black granite cracked by juniper roots,
the bark sloughed off, stumps twisted by winds.
Woodcarvers rub for weeks to groove the grain
that smooth—rings around wounds

grown perfect, curves no lathe could turn.
So many years, and no more friends come back.
I've been to the wall and rubbed my fingers on their names,
faces in polished granite. Now, we watch the dawn
and let the sun sustain us halfway between the Gulf of Mexico

and mountains. Nothing on these flat plains is like the war,
except sometimes asleep. Good neighbors offer fruit
from gardens on rationed water. Even our dogs
feel at home. They raise wet muzzles to the moon
and howl at stars so far away they stare.

TRAVELING IN PACKS

A splash, and sharp teeth drag the wildebeest
down, off balance, thrashing in slippery mud,
jerked to the churning foam of its own blood feast,
into the rushing river swollen by the flood,

kicked by the hoofs of wild-eyed others leaping
and splashing, the beast still kicking for breath,
but feebly, nearly paralyzed by fear and the death grip,
one crocodile thrashing to snap its neck,

tail flip and fangs sunk deeply into the throat
going under, dragging it into the darkest water
this wildebeest ever crossed, legs limp, as if floating,
coughing its goat-like bark under water,

the hungry herd scrambling up to the plains,
traveling in packs in the food chain,
a thunder of splashing hoofs and groans
over the swirl of bodies already bloated,

the bubble eyes of beasts like unexpected guests
with scales and appetites and tails, slowly
nosing upstream, without hurry,
choosing which one, which one is next.

AFTER THE LOST WAR

I buy my wife expensive vows that always start
I promise. I've promised to stop grumbling
about the past, neglecting her like bets I wad
and toss away. We've borrowed enough

to bail me out a thousand times, in hock
to a mob of apologies with flat noses
and pin-striped suits with guns. She locks
my fists with hers and kisses my eyelids open

so I can see. I pledged to take a vow
of poverty of rage, be baptized in faith
that all drivers aren't dying to drag race,
that I don't have to stomp the gas and frown

to keep all pickups with gun racks from passing.
I swore I'll stop planting weeds, not harvest
the same curved rows I own, sell the tractor,
let all my bones lie buried. I've promised

to let Saigon fall one last time tonight.
Stiff-necked, I lie with my head on her lap
and sigh. She bows between me and the light,
rubbing, rubbing my brow, my back.

THE MOVES A BODY MAKES

I like no wasted motion, prefer the blur
in the wings of hummingbirds, the splendor
of dump-truck drivers who know

when to tug the rope, all other jobs
hydraulic, the long bed tilting tons of dirt
then down, the slam and crash of rods

mechanical and tight. I like a riveter's
hard hat, its jaunty cock like Stetsons
on cowboys who ride bulls, no half-hearted

effort for eight seconds or all day.
Even now that I don't fly, I like a pilot's way
with thrust and ailerons, a dentist's

with a root canal, a blaster's thumb
and knuckles twisting dynamite in mountains.
Grandfather took two simple threads

and welded them with spit and fingers
to make a fly, tied for my sister
or for me. I like the skillful lift

and cleaning of two legs, my wife changing babies
again and again, showing me lift and turn,
skills of aeronautics in the home.

I like instructor pilots learning to let go,
my wife holding her hands away from toddlers
learning to wobble and walk or drive a car,

then waving goodbye until they disappeared.
I like how hard she buffs the porch swing's oak,
how long she holds her breath, and lets it out.

SONG FOR ONE-ARMED COWBOYS

for Jimmy

Take the reins in your teeth,
twirl rope with your only fist.
Let go and trust the coil. See it flick
quick as a snake's tongue
testing the wind for a feast.
When your horse jerks the calf
flat on its back with a thump,
spit out the reins and dismount,
bounding off balance to the calf
kicking to get up. Only your fist
can beat the calf and the doctor
who sawed off your helping hand
after the pickup crashed.
Feel the flank of the calf,
grab legs with the nub of your other
wrist and twist. Wrap once, twice
and leap back, stroll to the stands
with your hat off. Don't bother
about time or the trophy. Tonight
you ride for the brand.

AFTER THE FIRES
WE ONCE CALLED VIETNAM

Here on these flat fields I remember napalm,
that lavish charcoal lighter of a fat man's barbecue.
I'm like a pitcher with eyes in the back of his head
who wore his ball cap backward, ignoring the signs
his catcher gave, the finger between his thighs.
Often, he saw the runner leading too far off and whirled
and picked him off. Amazing, how hindsight made him hard
to steal on. He scrolled mistakes in his mind

like a three-inch roll of tape, adding them up,
the total always the same, like calling for a flyball
in the infield, *my fault, mine.* Saigon was lost
before I got there, fortunes stashed in Swiss banks,
French plantation rubber and raw silk. I flew off to war
and came back home alone. These are the facts.
I have a fence to mend, cattle to keep, or give up all
we've worked for. My wife depends on my saddle, ten miles

from any mesa, from any town, ten thousand miles
from jungles that once burned. Those villages were theirs,
and these flat pastures mine, a flat field not on fire
but shimmering in the sun, my herd of Angus burned
as black as toast in the sun that heats the wind,
that turns the windmill, that pumps cold water to the troughs
and faucet I bow to, splashing my face to cool my neck
until I'm sober. I know this patient Appaloosa is my horse,

those barbed wires sagging a mile away are mine,
and only I can twist and tighten them to save these steers
needing alfalfa and water from a well, not a lake
less tangible than guilt, a shimmer, a trick my eyes ignore
while I ride there on a trotting horse. The sun will blaze
tomorrow like most days on the plains, a mirage
fat Angus wade before the slaughterhouse. But now,
dismounting at the wires, when I glance back, it's gone.

A CABIN, EVEN A CAVE

Beyond that mountain where lightning flashed
last night, we'll find it. I want meat in the cabin,
elk or mule deer, big-horned sheep to shish-ka-bob
long winter nights. You want a deck surrounded by white
and purple columbine, a meadow without wild beasts,

even a cave. I want it all, blizzards, ten feet of snow.
Bring on the bears, the long-ribbed pumas blinking,
flicking dark-tipped tails, knowing we're here.
I want cold streams tumbling for miles over boulders,
cutthroat and Dolly Varden trout fighting the line,

and fire. You wish for eagles wheeling in the sky,
you want to see them hook and tumble love-locked,
a mile-long whirl of white, bald-headed sparks,
you want them loving every dangerous second
and saved. I'd settle for coyotes and hawks,

marmots and black squirrels flicking pompous tails.
We raised three babies on the plains, let go
and watched them walk, then fly away. They call
sometimes, like yodelers in mountains, seeing farther
than we can see and waving, turning, and going on.

LOSING IT AGAIN IN BOZEMAN

Once, in Bozeman, we saw the truck coming,
an Army convoy, a block of cars stopped
at the green light, state motorcycle cops
in boots and helmets looking back, revving,
ready to roar away. Then a flash of white
in the inside lane, old couple with faces cocked
so they could see. If they saw the cops,
they didn't believe, rolling past toward the light
at the legal speed. Ten thousand times
they'd stopped on red, but gone on through on green—
but not then, a blast of shattered glass and screams.
The truck hit like a boulder crashing through ice,

crushing the car like a beer can kicked,
tumbling and spinning. I saw steam, but did they die?
Maybe they weren't even rushed, taking their time
passing the last stalled car, hearing the click
of seams in the concrete, all of it orderly,
careful, believing in signs. I can't recall driving on,
not another block. What makes the mind go numb,
stumbling about in the dark? Files I want to retrieve
are locked, password denied. Trying to tap a nerve,
I think of Fred decades ago, flat on his face on the floor,
Montana hardwood holding him like a Tilt-a-Whirl,
the barkeep wiping his rag around as if he'd served

a thousand drunks. Why Bozeman? college boys
from Texas, hoping for summer work in Yellowstone.
I see a campus near the town, I smell cologne
but can't see faces, just names, *Fauncine* and *Joy.*
I don't know which I kissed, which one kneeled over
Fred, or left. I think that's how it happens, sudden
as a truck roaring with the right of way, or a drunk
in any town. I think I drove us back to Yellowstone,
but someone was lucky behind the wheel.
The jaws of life couldn't pry apart my mind,
that summer and that wreck. I think they died,
the flatbed loaded with tanks, the speed of steel

like a freight train. I remember a hubcap rolling
around and around like a roulette wheel,
like a hound whining, sniffing the street,
circling a turtle shut like a heart—the hubcap rolling
wire, wire wirewirewirewire and stopped,
the last sound I heard at the wreck, except steam.

EAST OF EDEN

Sometimes in mist I hear the hiss of snakes,
not scared or bitter, not out in cactus
rattlers feel cast to, but here by the lakes
and shade of far East Texas, dangerous,

mating in the shade of green magnolias
when dogwoods blossom and azaleas bloom.
This is the peace of pleasure, wet tundra
and spongy sky laced together, heirlooms

of tangled vines in mist before the waters
split into sky and dry land that first week.
This is the glimpse we saw, waking to ferns
and spongy loam decades ago in steamy Eden,

a dark garden of possibilities,
all jungle cats and honeymoon baboons
lounging at dawn, even the snakes. At ease
the heart hears itself, beating the old tattoo

of hunger and of hate. The eyelids blink
like sheaths of crocodiles, and one copper snake
slips beneath the silver ripple of the lake,
the gaudy body following itself until

it disappears, heading for us on the east shore
without a rock to grab for, without a club,
alone past middle age in the steamy downpour,
snakes along the far bank writhing in thunder,

coiling and uncoiling in lightning, most
slinking into the water, some into trees,
macaws and cheetahs screaming, stray goats
and panthers leaping, light flashing on teeth.

SLEEPING WITH THE ENEMY

They're back, the mad, back-scratching bullies.
I turn, shove up and sit. They vanish in chinks
and fissures of walls with almost audible noise.
Rockets no longer fall, no sweet gunpowder stink.
Saigon is gone, no longer named. Our boys
still sleep, no shouts or cartoons on TV.

And there, out there is the street we live on.
This is the floor my own feet touch, our phone
beside our bed. The joists are snug, the walls
and rafters. Our porch is pocked with holes,
the yard around the house. Men came with awls
and probed the wood and dirt, drilled concrete holes

in the porch, trenched down into the grass
but found no signs of termites. They shot the gas
and sealed the concrete plugs with hard epoxy
like armor I put on. My demons find all cracks,
but wood is a roof for our children's dreams.
Some nights I close my eyes, and if they're back,

they're tame, wart-faced, snarling hardly at all,
watching me twisted on my side, slack-jawed
and mild, if that's how I look without dreams.
Those nights, it's up to the sirens and cars
to shove me out to the harbor, under the screams
of wheeling gulls, the clatter of barges,

the stink of scows, love boats taking on wine
and diesel, peaceable kingdom of nighttime
without bats. Count on it, though, they need me
to stay alive, someone to torment with crimes
of flattery—swearing I deserve to see
unspeakable acts past corners of my mind,

to smell the bile and belly in their breath
puffed in the dark, to feel their bone-hooks
spreading my eyelids wide to watch their death,
to see what I really did, the fire I took,
my demons damned on the mountain, the holy bush
still burning, and me, about to look.

AGAIN THIS WINTER

Thousands of geese dropped down, squadrons
of perfect V's gliding over willows
without leaves. Back from Canada, they fanned out

over the grass, eating whatever geese eat
after thousands of miles on the flyway.
From the office, we saw them flocked in the park

like cobblestones. Families tossed scraps of bread,
surrounded. Toddlers turned their backs,
hands to their heads, gasping, begging for help.

After work, we crossed the hospital parking lot
and watched dogs parting the flocks,
their masters calling. Hundreds of geese

flapped away, but not far, banking back
to the lake, a mile of feathers and bowed necks
dipping and feeding, the whole world honking.

Across the road at the rest home, old people
in wheelchairs lined the sidewalks, wheels locked
and alone, or pushed by their children or aides.

Most pointed and waved. Some merely slumped,
heads bowed and limp, as if asleep,
now that they'd seen these wild, exotic wings.

THAT CHILD ABANDONED ON THE PORCH

In that child in tonight's newscast
I see our son, wandering Montana.
With luck, he'll find what he's missing,
hunting for gold or answers. What odds
brought him to us, a million to one,
ten million? The darkest hair, his eyes

squeezed tight in the agency's bright lights.
That nurse must have swaddled babies
a thousand times, but to us she was an angel
and we mere shepherds in from the cold.
There, near the gold-domed Denver capitol, star
on a highway map, there where they gathered taxes

in mountains, there we had come with nothing
but wads of paper telling us the birth hour,
not even the baby's weight, only that he
was the one, all of our luck in one boy,
and when we held him, he was,
he was the child in our arms.

HOW IT'S DONE

Lazy deer bend down black snouts
to grass. Dawn passed hours ago, and now,
like dominoes, the does fold
knobby toothpick legs and lie on slopes

we'd tumble down. Snowflakes flicker past,
no sounds, not even birds. From the back,
we watch the deer a hundred yards uphill,
and sip. Before the coffee's chilled,

one by one the does sprout legs
and rise. They arch their backs and stretch.
White tails flag rapidly twice—no danger,
yet, no scent they can't ignore, no hunger

they can't take with them as they twist
and wander off, nibbling this blade, this,
and this one, bowing to the bare
slopes farther on, whatever's there.

WHATEVER IT TAKES

You be a red fox in Rocky Mountain Park,
blackberries by every cave. I'll be the puma
cleaning his claws on a stump sheared off
by lightning, while black bears roam the tundra.
Dogs won't be allowed, not even on leash,
not even town dogs with the softest paws. Set free,
they'd sniff a frenzy of fox scent and dash
madly from their masters' cars, whining, brash
as blood hounds. I'll watch for them, gnawing on skulls,
lolling in boulders, flopping my three-foot tail:
let dogs bark themselves hoarse alone or in pairs,
let them scramble up rocks, let them come.

Beware the mean-hearted bear with cubs
deprived of easy pickings—no tents that spring,
the late snows deep. If shadows dark as dusk come
suddenly at noon, if slobbering she comes flinging
stones away from your lair, all fur and foul-breath
appetite, roaring and crashing inside, slip out
the crack of your cave only your nose can wedge.
In spite of a million acres of green to pounce
and glide through, in spite of laws against firearms,
we're on our own. Never mind the coyotes, mule deer
and elk everywhere, park wardens who set alarms
and lock themselves inside at night. After dark, my dear,

or all year long, we know what's here, stars
dotting the dark sky, bright sun or thunder.
I say it still, watch out: if whine or yard-dog
yapping drifts uphill where you rest, be ready to run,
be swift. That silence you hear between barks
might be me, crushed by a landslide or shot,
a poacher's steel-barbed arrow in my back. If dogs
run silently in packs to hem you in,
you be the fox, nimble and quick. If caught,
be snake, be a sleek black squirrel with dagger claws,
leap, climb any tree. If a fierce-eyed hawk
or eagle dives, you be the wind.

LEAVING THE SCENE

Sleet clicking in the trees, and finches flicking
maize and millet from the feeder. This late in spring,
and still the thin smoke whips from chimneys
a mile away. We rock and watch the dawn,
a ten-watt bulb beyond the clouds. Is all
this sideshow spring a barker's promise of warmth?
Our pears bloomed weeks ago, awnings of green
chiffon. The red oaks bulge, about to burst. Sleet
clicks like thousands of clocks ticking in our sleep.

We take turns leaving the scene with both mugs
to the kitchen for more, draining the urn,
the stiff steam bending as we straighten rugs
and weave back through forty years of furniture,
drapes opened, sleet beating a mute tattoo,
the old oaks wet and dark out to the pasture,
sleet on the steers' flat backs, bowing to dawn
and browsing, always grass and blocks of salt,
the sky nothing they ever watch, no matter what falls,
nothing fat cattle can't endure. We rock
and sip in silence, chairs turned to the porch,
grandchildren far away, knowing whatever force
is coming no one could stop, not even us.

Four

LEARNING HOW IN THE SOUTHWEST

PRAYING FOR RAIN ON THE PLAINS

If it comes,
let tractors stall hub-deep.
Pull off your boots and walk without socks,
squeeze globs of what you are. Feel mud like Vaseline,
the crushed and processed ferns and dinosaurs.
In a million years we'll ooze from vaults
and metal caskets, back in the mud where we belong.
Even West Texas dirt grows beans and cotton,
peppers that make us weep. Let rain come
by the bucket, let prices soar after floods,
let it hail. Pastors throughout the plains have prayed.
Farmers who sulk at home and tinker with plows
while their wives drive pickups to church,
even burned, skin-cancer atheists
stare at flat horizons without a cloud
and blink.

OLD PETS

Hawks in wide, hardscrabble skies track mice
in fields we say we own. We feed too many pets
our children raised by hand and abandoned.
Old bulls aren't worth the hay to save them,

but I don't throw away a glove because it's ugly.
Look at them, old goats and horses fat in the pasture.
That palomino's lame, the oldest mare on the plains,
drools when I rub her ear, can't hear unless I whisper,

leans on me like a post, slobbering oats from my glove,
swishing her tail. This abandoned barn was weeds,
the padlock missing. Thieves hauled good metal off,
nothing but someone's dream holding a roof over stalls,

the cows long slaughtered. Owls watched the plunder of doors
in silence. A man with children built this barn
to last, but not one stayed to carry on his herd.
We had to track them down to sign. And now the barn is ours,

and pastures fenced by barbed wires dangling from posts,
and most of those are broken. We might as well breed wolves
or trap for bounty snakes that kill our calves.
We could sell the rattlers' venom for research,

and wolves are bred for national parks in Montana
so why not here? Dawn, I shake my head at my schemes
and saddle up, time for rounding strays
and dumping hay to old pets bawling at the barn.

LEARNING HOW IN THE SOUTHWEST

Bring nothing clean. Fossils of the long dead
have burned, burned, and soot is king,
a fat voyeur that pries through your bags,
smudges like calling cards. This town is like Montana

only worse—no trees, no mountain streams,
no mountains. People here are loners and loud
for hours in bars for greasy steaks and company.
Hardhats from seven states drop by and brag

how many gushers they've drilled since Christmas,
baby's little booties encased in gold, not bronze.
The five best women here know secrets
no one wrestling derricks cares for

except after hours, down in motels
or trailers after the last bar closes,
after the last dull darts have hit
outside the target zone, the last fast women

with bleached hair and freckles have staggered off
with drunks who were their husbands after all.
That's when some mother's tunes drift
softly at midnight, alarming songs not taught

in oil fields, an ache for words that come
from more than the tongue, like honey
and homemade bread, learned when young,
commotion in the heart older than cactus

and black shale, a spark before the gas is capped—
music from school or church, poetry in motion
only such women give singing lullabies to babies
that cry and, cuddled, go back to sleep.

GARDENS OF SAND AND CACTUS

My wife takes salt for starters, and rusted strands
of barbed wire, the iron Grandfather left.
Chips chunks from a salt block mired in sand,
that tongue-rubbed marble artwork of the West,

anywhere cows roam—not buffaloes that lick
their salt from cactus and the bones of coyotes.
Takes bones, a skull, when she sees one. Takes snakeskin
like twisted strips of film. Looks under yucca

for the best, six feet at least. But fierce
grandfather snakes don't rattle until they're sure,
so she listens before she stoops. Finds horseshoes to pitch,
any flint or curved stone shaped like a tool.

Tugging our last child's Radio Flyer in the pasture,
brings pigments back, even the burnt sienna bolus
of owls. Scrapes umber from banks of the Brazos,
however dry, gold dust where bobcats marked the stumps.

Packs, stacks it all. Takes time, fans with her hat,
then hauls that wagon wobbling to our house.
Amazed that she makes gardens of cactus and sand,
I miter frames to hang whatever she's found

and salvaged as art, even rocks she cuts and tumbles
in a barrel grinding like sweet, hand-cranked ice cream,
turning this desert we call home into babies' mobiles,
wind chimes and swings, bird feeders in every tree.

WEEDING THE STRAWBERRY GARDEN

Flashes of light and thunder,
then splashes of rain, then rain
as loud and steady as faith
if faith had sound. That's prayer
in the garden, chopping the crust

with steel prongs delicate as lace,
pulling out weeds like needles,
strawberries sour and green.
Another week, they'll all be there
if sassy crows stay away.

Sherlock looks down with prune eyes
plastered in clay, face scowling
even at me. Crucified, hung out
to dry day and night, he holds both
broom-stick arms like a child, *this* wide—

a patched scarecrow savant I offer
like a lightning rod. If thunder comes,
let the steep slope flood.
I merely plant and hoe,
chop clods like brittle leather

so earth can soak. Let it soak
all week to the roots of berries.
All autumn we'll share the berries
that survive with our neighbors—
not hoarding the fruit they bore

for we have more than we could eat
preserved from last year's crop,
pressure-cooked, pressed down,
running over, this plot of earth
still fertile, the lightning almost here.

WHERE THE FENCE GOES

A Walkman on my belt kept time
with four iron shoes, my sorrel trotting
along the barbed wire, miles of sand.
Even a gliding hawk knew music

beamed like heat waves under the prairie sun.
Fiddles filled my mind, the whine of steel guitars
and blondes who sang me full of blues,
the color of skies that wide. The horse's neck

kept lifting up and down, like prancing.
I rode where the fence failed, wires that snapped,
posts shoved to the ground by hunters.
How many times had I patched those miles,

how many trucks had I loaded with steers?
Easy, before our son went off to the Army.
I didn't listen to news out there
with only a horse for a partner.

Our son was safe, or he was when he wrote
weeks before from the Persian Gulf. Most days
I found all fences tight, except for one post
broken, dangling from barbed wires.

Buzzards kept their own curfew and rhythm,
always aloof. Often I saw them
gliding a wide, slow spiral. Hawks
went their own way, alone, not needing a man

and his rifle. After I fed the horse
at dusk, all music off, I watched the news,
too far from the war to solve it,
too many boys on TV to ignore.

IN GUSTY WINDS THAT WILD

Hawks don't hunker down in burrows
when it blows. Their claws dig hard
on posts against stiff wind.
Sand gashes the skin like glass.
People pop their contacts out
and weep the scratches clean.

Hawks on barbed wires bob
and ride it out, beaks to the wind,
wings tight as if diving. In April,
wind pounds daily from the west.
Nothing flies in gusty winds that wild,
not even hawks. Like that one

across the road, caught
near our mailbox. Here,
squeeze the binoculars
and watch those feathers flounce.
Watch the claws, that splendid head.
His eyes don't even blink.

JOGGING WITH OSCAR

When I take my dachshund jogging, boys and widows gawk
and stop tossing balls or lopping limbs off shrubs. They call
and point at long, pot-bellied Oscar trotting like a rocker horse,
tongue wagging, dragging on grass when he hops over skateboards,

long muzzle wide as if laughing, eager, sniffing the breeze.
All Oscar needs is a tree like a mailbox, postcards from dogs
he barks at at night, and odd whiffs he can't place. When he stops
and squats, up runs a neighbor's collie tall as a horse,

stalking like a swan meeting an eel, muzzle to muzzle in dog talk,
collie tail like a feather fan. Wherever we go, we're not alone
for an hour, devoted hobblers on the block, the odd couple—
long-legged bony man jogging along, obeying the leash law,

the black, retractable nylon sagging back to Oscar, who never balks
or sasses when I give the dangling leash a shake, but trots to me
desperate for affection, panting like a dog off to see Santa,
willing to jog any block for a voice, a scratch on the back.

I've seen that hunger in other dogs. I watched my wife
for forty years brush dogs that didn't need the love he does.
When my children visit, my oldest grandsons trot with him
to the park, that glossy, auburn sausage tugging and barking,

showing off. The toddlers squat and pat him on his back.
They touch his nose and laugh, and make him lick them on the lips.
Good Oscar never growls, not even if they fall atop him.
He was a gift from them, last Christmas, a dog their pop

could take for walks and talk to. Oscar would have loved my wife,
who spoiled and petted our old dogs for decades, coaxing them up
for tidbits on the couch beside her, offering all the bliss
a dog could wish for, a hand to lick, a lap to lay their heads.

Oh, he's already spoiled, barks at bluejays on his bowl,
fat and lonely unless I'm home. But how groomed and frisky
he could be if she were here, how calm to see us both
by the fire, rocking, talking, turning out the lights.

For Grandfather,
in memory of Grandmother Anna

SYMPATHY

My wife fattens scrapbooks with facts of someone's death
or wedding whose parents made West Texas home—
classmates, aunts or daughters of distant cousins' friends.
She knows them all, I marvel, watching her scan.
With blunt steel shears, she snips obituaries,
clippings she'll send in sympathy cards or save

or take with casseroles or cakes. She reads the news
like crossword puzzles or rosaries, and sighs
or shakes her head. My wife recycles pounds of paper,
columns and dates cut out, the pages dangling.
She knows that puzzles are only puzzles, that wisdom
is different from facts, that even wisdom can't save us.

Our bookshelves sag. A hundred horses died
to make the glue it takes to stick the dead
and married in, a random history of people
she met some time and loved or heard of, all names
important to her, worth keeping track of, even on pulp
that yellows and burns, she knows, even as she clips.

IN DICKEY COUNTRY

for James Dickey

Jim said travel's a mean canoe trip
down a river about to be dammed,
home a bow and arrows ready,
a good dog sleeping at your feet.
Memory is Doris Holbrook's wrench
and a well-oiled Harley for a getaway.

Life is a trap and always short
and often ugly, if you're a lifeguard
and the boy drowns when you're not around.
We're all drowning with others
and all we can do is try to save someone
another hour, maybe by the highway,

your own boy maddened by bees.
Odd things happen, sleeping out at Easter
or in the mountain tent, hunting relics
at battlefields and finding *fathers,*
fathers. Always, in masks like armor
or in the common grave, they wait,

all living and long-gone heroes
and out-of-shape runners wildly connected,
only one leap to beyond-reason gold,
one sip from a helmet for the last brief hope
of another, who died as we all must come
to our last performance, having done

all we can do, kneeling down by our hacked,
glittering graves, under pressure,
or in amazing armor we put on
when we begin living forever, falling
in the dark without a parachute, calling
with our last few feet of breath for God.

VOICES ON JUKEBOX WAX

Pulling our Stetsons low, we whispered songs
to sweethearts who clung so close we danced
in slow motion, heartache of steel guitars,
vows we swore with our bones. Their hair was the air
for an hour. We breathed and held them close,
ignoring the war for the night, voices
on jukebox wax winding around like a rope.
One week we kissed them hard and rode off,

swearing we'd bring back silk and souvenirs.
Long after a war no one we cared for
survived without scars, Earl and I are here
with wives as old as country songs and guitars,
our children older than all of us that fall.
Don's a name on a wall in Washington.
I hear his name sometimes in questions
at class reunions. I haven't heard from Carl.

CATARACTS

Clouds over Long's Peak, blue sky everywhere but there,
and when I glance away and back, they're gone. Imagine:
I make the highest mountain disappear by tipping my head,
shifting my cataract eyes. Watch that herd of mule deer

on the slope, floppy ears like semaphore: gone, a blur
like TV reception in the fifties. When I blink left
or right, they're back, magic. In night flight,
they taught that staring at a light too long

would saturate the rods or cones, a blind spot
we could find by sweeping left to right like radar.
A few more years, the doctor will pluck them out
like pearls, *presto,* bringing my vision back

like a picture tube, the world once more in focus.
If it works, that is, no procedure perfect.
Here from the cabin deck, I watch the river
cascade left to right, flowing to nothing but a roar,

then a shimmer twisting away downhill. For years,
we watched our son come rafting by with his friends,
a bucking, rubber float jolting them into shrieks, so close
we could snap them as they passed, mouths open, holding on

in white-water rapids flinging them hard downriver
past the trees. I've turned old photo albums right to left,
a blur of portraits and snapshots. I've helped my wife
tidy his room, storing trophies, giving away good clothes.

I watched the car towed back, glass and metal
mangled out of focus, a scarred blur almost a car
that didn't burn. I've been to the scene, walked down
the ledge and lowered myself by roots and boulders

where his car careened. I've stood there where it crashed.
I've turned my eyes as far as I could see downstream,
even twisted in my chair, thinking I heard
his voice behind me, not merely the river's roar.

FOR GOD IN MY SORROWS

Now on the highway, the dwindling traffic, a leaky faucet of lights
after midnight. I try to ignore the stars, a billion witnesses
that I give myself to black skies, not even gravity holding me back,
cast into outer darkness. Not stars always on fire, not fire,

but beyond, whatever scattered them: *that* power. I've seen
the world on fire, from bunkers, each man alone, hunkered down
at night to survive the sirens. Not fire, not the natural world
that burns and bloodies us in wars or car wrecks, hurtling out there

even now behind headlights—or on foot at noon, distracted,
crossing the road and crushed, like road kill. Black night
has answers I don't want. But after stars collapse,
after all that mass snuffs out like a match, after whatever

Peter meant by the known world melting with fervent heat,
how much remains? That's what I miss here on the plains
a mile from the highway, cars and trucks like falling stars,
hardly a roar. Do those black skies have answers after all,

terror no less than daylight, night vision blinded by the star
we'll never see at this distance? Is it blackness I seek,
after all, total loss, like turning my back on the highway
and shutting my eyes tight as if those billion fires were gone,

leaving me free to pray without the crutch of fire,
not even flashlights? What, beyond wars and weapons, beyond stars,
what could I find? The light that guided wise men?
No, that's done and over, servant of the source I yearn for.

Astronomers call it no star at all, scoffing. I believe
as I know my hand is here before me in the dark, my eyes
stretched wide—sun, moon and stars almost forgotten—
I feel faith inches away from my face, thumb and split claws

cunningly made to hold a rope or grope along the wall at night
for a light switch. When I close my eyes, magically,
it's here. This, this is what I need, without lights or cities
man-made and dying, somehow to know I'm known.

FISHING WITH UNCLE WALTER
IN WORLD WAR II

I remember the first tub of red racers I saw in a walled shed
in Arkansas, down by the Ouachita. My uncle led us there
when I was nine, Grandfather and a man with some 4-F condition
or too old. We drove five hundred miles in World War II
over bumpy roads at night to see my aunt and uncle

who lost their only son at Pearl Harbor, to grieve again
about what happened two years ago, to fish the river
Grandfather trawled and trapped when he was a boy in poverty
  Arkansas,
his daddy dead, his scattered brothers fretting for their boys
flung out across the world like dice and black bones,

a mystery of fate. My father was in jungles of Guam
or Saipan, pinheads on a map my mother kept. But here was rot,
real darkness in some back-swamp bait shop, a dozen wash tubs
of rotting crawdads, eels, and fish heads, the hot shed
squishing under my Keds as I ducked in mud under cobwebs

long as nets. My uncle punched me in the ribs and kidded
what my girl friends would think of this. I mumbled something
and my uncle laughed. What all this rot and splash of slime
in barrels had to do with fish I didn't know, the perch and bass
we caught back on the Brazos suckers for worms and grubs

the size of snot. I wondered if this was one of those places
we whispered about at night behind the barn, where men
went to women, where boys were lucky if they came back alive,
bleeding, part of their things chopped off, circumcised
or sick for weeks. I shuddered, that odd, familiar swelling

in my pants and taste of alum. Grandfather walked behind me
like a guard, and I followed my distant uncle and a one-armed man
who hobbled to a row of tubs and buckets. *My God,*
my Uncle Walter said, stepping back and clapping
as if he'd found the manger, always one to make the best

of everything. I stopped nose level with the tub, nothing
but fifty pounds of straw and dirt. Grandfather bowed down to
    smell,
big-knuckled fists on the nicked and rusted rim. The one-armed
    man
who owned it all reached around my back and tapped the tub
with a hammer. Chaos swarmed, enormous worms twelve inches
    long,

swirling out of black dirt and squirming over each other,
gone in the blink of my eyes, the fastest motion I'd ever seen.
His nub still around me, the unshaved owner banged again,
and out they wound and slithered, red racers fat and slimy naked.
I imagined the fish these would catch, the sharks or alligator gar

it would take to swallow them, the meat hooks we'd have to squish
and impale them on, if any of us could hold them writhing
like fire hoses. I don't know how many gar and big-mouthed bass
we caught that week, what bait we used. I remember my uncle
suddenly weeping against the wall, sunlight odd on his balding head

in the baitshop. I remember Grandfather clearing his throat
and staring at worms with unusual interest, big knuckles white
on the tub. Now that I've been to war, now that I've watched TV
around the clock and worried about one son under Iraqi rockets,
I can hear my Uncle Walter beating his fist against the wall

of that bait shop, there to fish with only his brother
and a distant nephew. I can't remember much about that day,
but Grandfather's face sunburned. Out on the lake, I drank
my first half-bottle of beer. I got to pee from the boat,
standing up, a long-arched splash and ripple my uncle promised

would draw fish. I know we carried two canoes over a crust
of mud that shuddered like dough, and fished the river
past midnight. I remember Uncle Walter cursing, clubbing
alligator gars with his oar, trash fish he hated, head down,
shaking, smashing them in the moonlight with his fists.

FATHERS AND SONS

I rattle the porch as I walk, closing the screen door softly,
guided by the coffee pot's red light. Quietly,
I fill the china cup, a gift from my wife, still sleeping.
Four, no, five A.M., the clock's red digits say. Pace if I must,
but on the porch, far enough away from the bedroom

so I won't wake her, if I don't knock the cup off,
hunched at the screen still blue, waiting like me
for words that shoved me out of bed at three. Outside,
I hear crickets as if there's not a screen between us.
Cicadas have been quiet for hours, no barking dogs,

no trucks on the highway miles away, or I can't hear them.
I haven't heard a coyote since midnight, no owls,
nothing but crickets and the computer's hum, and this porch
that creaks and rattles when I pace, thinking of something
to write our oldest son overseas, a rapid force of soldiers

in the hills of Bosnia. In Desert Storm, he was out of touch
for weeks when nothing, not even a phone call or a fax,
could find him. My father died in battle so his sons
would never fight, far off on Guam and Saipan,
island hopping with MacArthur. Where I went is a footnote

in history books, stacks of facts we compiled about a war
already being lost, stored in a vault in Saigon
until someone shredded and burned them, pulling out.
I see blurred silhouettes of trees in the east.
I write about those trees, the crickets. I make up jets

overhead, letting down from Dallas. I lie about coyotes,
claiming they're back, howling the way our boy heard them
in these fields a thousand times. I say his mother's up,
here on the porch, sipping her second cup. I say
she sends her love, which is no lie. I say she'll write

tomorrow. I ask *How are you,* but delete that,
add something about the crops, the herd bull's shoulder
he hurt butting the barn. I go back inside for a cup,
and pace the porch until the sun is up. I close
with *Love,* and sign it, all my hand can do.

Five

THE WALTZ WE WERE BORN FOR

WHEN THE CHILDREN HAVE GONE

How many elk and deer roam down to crop the leaves
we water in drought, to lick salt blocks we haul
from town and scatter? We chart all elk we see,
even bulls with bad reputations, awkward in collars
park rangers strapped around stiff necks, antlers sawed off.
Those go with the herd like wethers, marked by dollops

of paint. Some years, some come bleeding, ears chewed off
by coyotes bold as bears that tourists with cameras hunt.
Our children named all babies in the herd. In fall,
bulls learning to bugle bluff their way to rut.
Pictures help us say, *Look at that, there's Shorty—*
a rack of antlers taller than his pa's. They strut

downtown, stalling traffic, a glut of elk and offspring.
Not even grain we plant could save them, not trees they break
by crushing down our fence. We wouldn't want them pitiful
and tame. We clean up gladly after elk each year,
knowing they'll leave, never nod their racks as if thankful,
slow and clumsy in our garden, graceful on the hills.

CATCHING MY GRANDSON

Oh, look, old Galileo whispered, *look, we move.*
And burning, burning in the sky, the sun stood still.
Earth turned and spun and whirled about the ball,
but no one else believed. Not then. *Take time,*

Grandfather called, watching our first adopted toddler fall,
push up and waddle to my lap. *It goes so fast.*
Yeah, yeah, I thought, patting my daughter's goldilocks,
thumbing her tears away. I loved that chubby cherub

with the grapejuice grin, took turns changing Pampers,
scrubbing that kid in bubble baths, giving time
and horsey rides, a thousand tasks each day before I slept.
I accuse myself, I confess I doubted that old man.

What passes fast, I thought, was time enough to do
what must be done—another flight, reports overdue,
the grass I had to cut. The earth does turn,
no, spins. I crouch now, catching my grandson

firing the ball, the red seams spinning.
He's older than his mother was that night
Grandfather called, when my knees could duckwalk a mile,
my shoulders and biceps bulged. *Ouch,* I mutter, now,

a pain each time I lob the baseball back,
my right arm stiff, the shoulder bony,
the hard ball wobbling, plopping in his glove.
And how he burns it back, curve ball inside

I have to dive for, falling again for physics
faster than reflex, and I'm laughing on the ground,
hugging the ball, my grandson laughing,
staggering off the mound, pounding his glove.

ANNIVERSARY: ONE FINE DAY

Who would sit through a plot as preposterous as ours,
married after years apart? Chance meetings may work
early in stories, but at operas, darling, in Texas?
A bachelor pilot, I fled Laredo for the weekend,
stopping at the opera from boredom, music I least expected.
Of all the zoos and honky-tonks south of Dallas,
who would believe I would find you there on the stairs,

Madame Butterfly about to start? When you moved
four years before, I lost all hope of dying happy,
dogfighting my way through pilot training, reckless,
in terror only when I saw the man beside you.
I had pictured him rich and splendid in my mind
a thousand times, thinking you married with babies
somewhere in Tahiti, Spain, the south of France.

When I saw the lucky devil I hated—only your date,
but I didn't know—he stopped gloating, watching you wave,
turned old and bitter like the crone in *Shangri La*.
Destiny happens only in plays and cheap movies—
but here, here on my desk is your photo, decades later,
and I hear sounds from another room of our house,
and when I rise amazed and follow, you are there.

GRANDFATHER'S POCKET WATCH

Sequoias can't tell time until they're dead.
Cut down, they tell their age, confessions at the stake
before they burn. Counting rings, we marvel,
knocking on hardwood. We stack fresh cords
against the barn, but find logs dark next fall,

the slow inferno of decay. I thought
this hardwood deck Grandfather built would last.
I handed nails across and watched his big arm
pound the hammer down. Now, nothing stops the rot,
not even sealants. New planks I've fitted in

are flat, mismatched, a patchwork of old boards
that splinter, have to be ripped for firewood.
Grandfather got this watch for forty years' hard work—
a handshake from his boss, a watch fob and a plaque.
Retired, he took it out sometimes and stared at it

and rocked. It dangles by a chain above my desk,
the monotony of *tock-tick-tock* hypnotic.
I miss his big-boned callused hands,
the way he wound the stem till it was tight,
the way he held it to my children's ears.

STONES GRANDFATHERS CARVED

So this is where great uncles yowled their vowels
and raised cathedrals coal smoke turned to tar
but bombs did not dislodge. Windows leaded tight
still fit, and gargoyles scowling at my Texas drawl
leer down and wink. Cathedrals bulge with tourists

faithful to stone walls. The Thames flows slowly
and the buses roar. No one is timid
in these left-hand lanes. Hard to believe
plague stalked these streets. Here they killed a king
and laughed at slobbering Swift in Bedlam.

Is London burning? Do natives over fifty
still hear buzz bombs in their sleep? Is the blitz
handed down like titles, like the Tower
and chopping block? They still ride after foxes,
open castles to tourists who swat at aphids

trapped in tapestries. Last night, a woman in a flat
leaned out, dreaming of fame in this realm
of masonry, gauze curtains flapping in the heat.
Last week at Gatwick, a man with nose rings
and magenta hair strutted the terminal

banging a drum, no longer novel in a city sober
as its name, thousands of actors writing plays,
always a tower announcing London time. Tonight,
I'll lift a glass to masons I never knew,
eroded dates and names I found on English stones.

TWINS AND ORAL HISTORY

If you think ground squirrels are fun,
wait till you see a coyote.

I'd never say that to grandsons,
but even coyotes have to eat. So what do I tell
their taped school project tomorrow?
What idealistic teacher makes historians of kids
in the second grade? With a flourish of her tongue

and simple Xeroxed lists of questions,
she'll flick us back to Saigon or Da Nang,
memories static as paper weights with winter scenes.
What did you do in the war, Grandpa? Shake us
with cassette tapes and watch snow flurries swirl.

What do I say about native kids their age?
They were hungry but cute, with tangled hair and eyes.
Did they play? Yes, I think they ran a lot. No,
they didn't believe in Santa Claus, but Halloween
was all year long. The tarmac track where I jogged

outside Saigon was hot. Yes, I sunburned
and others, most in jogging shorts and tennis shoes
or boots. No, I killed nobody on the track.
No, men jogged in the jungle with back packs
and rifles. No, boys, I never saw tigers

eating people on the battlefield,
but if your teacher's daddy was there,
I guess they did. No, I don't have a gun to show you,
no enemy's teeth or dried ears in my duffle bag.
Have I been back to Vietnam? Do I have nightmares

still? [What's next on this teacher's list?
Have you stopped beating Grandma?]
It was a long time ago, and boys, you know
what happens when you sleep. You never know
what might trot by inside your mind—a friend

from school who moved away you'll never see
again, a tiger in a Disney show, a coyote
gnawing on a bone. But that's enough. Come,
hug me, both of you, then race me to the swing set
before your mother calls us to wash up.

THE WAR IN BOSNIA

Under darkness of stars our son flies
over Bosnia, keeping watch over snow.
Apache gunships will be out tonight.

The moon on foreign snowfields highlights
bodies running under trees, friend or foe.
Under darkness of stars our son flies

with star scope and rockets and wide eyes
over war zones bitter enemies know.
Apache gunships will be out tonight.

What keeps a nation armed and justifies
air power is such a killing field—we know,
but under darkness of stars our son flies.

In boots and parka, someone watches the skies
and owns disposable Stingers, and is cold.
Apache gunships will be out tonight.

I conjure God to stop him, warp his sights.
I stare with the prayer all fathers know.
Under darkness of stars our son flies.
Apache gunships will be out tonight.

RIVER OF THE ARMS OF GOD

She's learning to cope with mud I track back
from the Brazos, bearing cards stamped upside down
by grandkids, smudged, sometimes a Crayola clown
our pre-school ballerina drew. So this is the way
we grow old, absent-minded clown tracking enough fish scales
and dust to make our porch a garden, and grandmother
picking up needles from haystacks of our lives,

ignoring stiff knuckles, stitching Raggedy Ann
and Andy out of scraps. She crochets clothes for dolls
and wanders humming through the house. Stares at the phone,
the walls, knits shawls for widows she inherits,
her aunts and in-laws. I've seen her rub and rub her knees
when she thought I nodded off. Sometimes I feel it, too,
out in the shop, carving, trying to make a block of oak

say *hawk* or *robin*. Hooks rust like old men's hairy ears,
and rods turn stiff as knees. Buckets of week-old minnows
feed spiders spinning webs like fish nets in the barn,
and stringers dangle like keys to forgotten locks.
Let the ones that got away brag about how I lost,
and spawn in eddies like muddy legends after floods.
I've stopped keeping count of the Brazos's bounty,

River of the Arms of God all we need for now.
Red wine with beef is the menu, and fish any month
from the Brazos, slabs of catfish or bass thick as my thumb.
It's all in the name the Spaniards gave, *Rio de los Brazos
del Dios,* crossing themselves on the plains,
kneeling by muddy banks that led them stumbling in armor
on starving horses back to their ships and home.

Our children far away are older than we were
when we drove here and unloaded, propped up
a sagging barn and planted oats and alfalfa,
dug post holes deep enough to hold a herd,
patting each other's hands till midnight by the fire,
our children bathed and put to bed upstairs,
winter storms far off, the dry heat easy to ignore.

BLESSINGS THE BODY GAVE

All week the river rolled
down a fancy rickrack of stones,
a mountain roar. Even the dog heard music,
static of a battery radio. Sprawled,
the dog kept time with worried eyes.

He believed that cabin was home,
if we said so, the air so thin it froze.
Last week we stuck in mountain mud, slick-spinning
down to stone until wet rubber smoked.
Nothing could turn us back from an A-frame

high in the San Juan. We waded the last half-mile
to blue spruce dwarfing a red asbestos roof.
All night the dark clouds rained a roar
and far from telephones. All week, we tamped
pine needles and leaned back, propping pads

on laps of drawn-up legs. Sunlight sliced
through vinegar-sweet pine needles, our fingers
sketching nothing tame, the leaves so still
we heard tapping and scratching
like two of everything approaching to be named.

Last night, I dragged our chairs to the hearth
and scratched a long-stemmed match. Music
hummed and buzzed, static as the searching dial
spun slow. Her hands knew all the songs
I needed, and she twisted distant stations off,

our last hours alone in the mountains.
I leaned my rawhide chair to hold her,
the pine logs popping sparks. She rubbed
my flannel sleeves and we locked hands and rocked,
the cabin cold unless we faced the fire.

WILD DUCKS FLOATING BY

Under spruce trees with roots dangling from a cutbank,
under the thunder, our last son slumbers in a tent
on public land in Montana. A river flows by his flap
with trout and sometimes trees: it is swift, here,

millions of years deep. He thinks among these weeds,
sits on this stump and strums to nothing but stars.
We've come to see where he shaves and sleeps.
I watched old Uncle Bob crawl in a car

crammed with junk and blankets, his only home.
Joe won't come home, won't finish school.
Hand to mouth, my father called all hoboes
who almost starved before World War II.

I touch his mountain bike's worn tires
and wonder how he'll cross the continent again,
what drives him away from roofs and indoor fires,
taking odd jobs for peanut butter and bread.

He hangs his clothes on a pole to dry,
splattered with house paint, torn and sewn,
dozens of butts crushed by the campfire,
his only stove that circle of stones.

I can't stand this loud river without a sky,
even all these trout and trees, these wild ducks
floating by. Tomorrow we'll hold him tight
when we leave, rubbing his black, wiry stubble,

his arms and shoulders hard, without a wife,
alone in a tent in a forest. Slowly we'll back away,
drive out on the winding highway and wave
to him by his river swiftly out of sight.

ALL WE DO IS ALREADY HISTORY

We're all on a speeding Amtrak,
one-way tickets toward glittering
far-off events, no turning back.
Whatever we do, it's already history.

Queue up in the terminal and board
when they call our names,
it's all over—the thrill of *"All aboard,"*
anticipation we could almost taste.

Pastures and valleys we glimpse
are Switzerland clacketing by,
destinations we'd like to visit,
but railway warnings flash by,

cars waiting, people waving in their fields,
then gone. We're pulling emergency cords
and calling, hauling the conductor here
to our window—*There, those resorts*

are our stop. He jerks away
and scowls. We look back, frantic,
but it's gone, the end of our holiday,
our foreheads mashed against the glass.

For days, for years, we can taste
the legendary cones of Cornish cream,
hear the crack of the bat that day
in Yankee stadium, peanuts and memories,

boyish, broad-shouldered Mickey Mantle
rounding the bases, doffing his cap
as he jogged home and down into the dugout,
another man at bat.

ALONE IN THE TUNDRA

Marmots flop in the sun and scratch, face-down on lichen
plastered to rocks. Tundra is a jungle of blooms and vines
thin as an eyelash. Here, the heart skips, breath too cold
for rattlers coiled like tribal gods under boulders.

Snowplows cleared the road last week, winding past cliffs
a thousand feet straight down. Curves meet themselves uphill,
mountains falling away for miles. Here's where we'd live,
if they'd let us, west of Estes Park. Before Bunker Hill,

these flowers sprouted in topsoil thin as skin. Tundra
grows under snow, releasing oxygen, one molecule a month.
But it's April, all pastel and bees—not bumblebees
with heavy chests, lazy in meadows miles below, but bees

the size of gnats that float and fumble the tundra's pollen,
turning bantam blossoms into seeds. Buck-toothed marmots
look up, no lack of weeds to feed on. Now we're alone,
out of breath in the tundra, oddly giddy, our children grown.

We kneel like Gulliver to bring exotic worlds to us,
mauve and olive forests no taller than our thumbs. We breathe
this aroma of ferns, fighting an impulse to pick these weeds
and vines stuck together like velcro, to taste the buds,
red dots of blooms so small we need a microscope to see.

TO HAVE AND TO HOLD

Didn't they enter that marriage forever,
didn't they though? To have and to hold each other
forever, forsaking all men in tuxedos
and elegant maidens waiting to catch the bouquet,
so clever to know it would last. Some friends
seem to say that, sadly or grandly at parties
and ballrooms, always surprised that it lasted
this long. We calm them and offer our toasts
to their brides or new grooms at receptions
with strangers and blooms like bouquets.
Years are like dances with friends changing hands,
new partners for foxtrots or waltzes,
or sitting it out. We're oddly off-guard
when they ask us to dance, odd couple oddly regarded
like wallflowers or parents, quaint chaperons
at mixed-family reunions, monogamous dinosaurs
back from the tar pits, quaint and club-footed—
how charming like sophomores, possessive
or scared, how daring like monks to love only one
or to grow old together thinking it's so. They watch us
for chinks in our armor, flirtations and waves.

Oh, he's the sly one, they probably say—
forsaking all others, ha, that'll be the day.
They watch her for bruises, for a drugged,
glassy gaze. Our children have babies
that hurry us dizzy from birthday to birthday,
already almost our age when we married—*always*
now down to decades or days. We're aging
amazed and surprised by how swiftly it passes,
no turning back—how awful, how destined, I see,

to leave her alone with my name behind deadbolts—
or worse, and unbearably so, to lose her
someday, not ever to hold her, not touch
that remarkable face, splotched with age spots.
How could I stand it, to suffer her gone,
not hear her call me, with gray in her hair,
not ever to rise and build fires for her early
or listen to jays in the garden at dawn.

WHERE BUFFALO GRASS GROWS LOUD
IF WE LISTEN

Out here, cactus is the skyline, a hundred miles of flat.
Turn in a circle and never know you're back,
except for the neighbor's ranch, barns like specks of mica
in the dust, his windmill a semaphore for water, *Home*.

Deep forests are a myth, black loam and heritage and trees.
The one road into town has highway signs boys use
as targets. The asphalt's cracked, dandelions thriving
as if crews planted them. Rattlesnakes nap

on the shoulders, no trucks along for months.
Jackrabbits limp along like dogs, nibbling grass
and careless weeds, no need to hurry from nothing
that can hide. Slumped on an aging Appaloosa,

I roll a smoke that may take half a day to lick,
to get it right. I dig in deep shirt pockets for a match,
and bite it like a toothpick. I stick the unlit
cigarette like a feather in my hat. I kicked the habit

four years ago after the last grassfire
some trucker started. The butt's for practice,
in case I'm ever bored. My wife saves rattles
for the grandkids, flint arrowheads she finds,

digging strawberry gardens, prying out rocks
for the fish pond, scooping iron and umber
for sand paintings on the patio. Rocking at dusk
that starts at dinnertime and lasts past Halloween,

we talk softly about a coyote a mile away,
one drop of water bulging at sundown from a pipe
over the brimming-full horse trough, the stretch
and shimmer of the drop before it falls.

THE WALTZ WE WERE BORN FOR

Wind chimes ping and tangle on the patio.
In gusty winds this wild, sparrow hawks hover
and bob, always the crash of indigo
hosannas dangling on strings. My wife ties copper
to turquoise from deserts, and bits of steel
from engines I tear down. She strings them all
like laces of babies' shoes when the squeal
of their play made joyful noise in the hall.

Her voice is more modest than moonlight,
like pearl drops she wears in her lobes.
My hands find the face of my bride.
I stretch her skin smooth and see bone.
Our children bring children to bless her, her face
more weathered than mine. What matters
is timeless, dazzling devotion—not rain,
not Eden gardenias, but cactus in drought,
not just moons of deep sleep, not sunlight or stars,
not the blue, but the darkness beyond.

The Ohio State University Press/*The Journal* Award in Poetry
David Citino, Poetry Editor

1997	Judith Hall	*Anatomy, Errata*
1996	John Haag	*Stones Don't Float: Poems Selected and New*
1995	Fatima Lim-Wilson	*Crossing the Snow Bridge*
1994	David Young	*Night Thoughts and Henry Vaughan*
1993	Bruce Beasley	*The Creation*
1992	Dionisio D. Martínez	*History as a Second Language*
1991	Teresa Cader	*Guests*
1990	Mary Cross	*Rooms, Which Were People*
1989	Albert Goldbarth	*Popular Culture*
1988	Sue Owen	*The Book of Winter*
1987	Robert Cording	*Life-list*

The George Elliston Poetry Prize

1987	Walter McDonald	*The Flying Dutchman*
1986	David Weiss	*The Fourth Part of the World*
1985	David Bergman	*Cracking the Code*